D0803130

HOW DO I
DEAL
WITH MY
EMOTIONS?

JOHN RAGSDALE

SMITH
FREEMAN
Publishing

ABOUT THE AUTHOR

John Ragsdale is a husband (to Kristin), a daddy (to Evan and Davis), a lover of Jesus, a singer-songwriter, a passionate communicator, and pastor of The Hills Nashville.

CONTENTS

A MESSAGE TO READERS

How do I deal with my emotions? It's an easy question to ask, at least in theory. But, it's a much more difficult question to answer when your emotional thermostat is running very hot or very cold. The ideas in this book can help you learn to deal with those roller-coaster emotions that, if left unchecked, threaten to upset your psyche or derail your day. This text does not attempt to answer every question concerning your particular personality or your specific situation. Instead, it gives you time-tested, biblically based strategies for addressing troublesome feelings.

Each day, you must make countless choices that can bring you closer to God or not. When you guard your heart by guarding your emotions—and when you live by the principles contained in God's Word—you will inevitably earn His blessings. But if you make unwise choices—or if you allow negative emotions to hijack your thoughts—trouble is just around the corner.

Would you like to improve the quality of your day and your life? Then guard your heart above all else. When you're tempted to speak an unkind word, hold your tongue. When you're tempted to strike out in anger or act impulsively, slow down and talk things over with God. When you're uncertain of your next step, follow in the footsteps of Jesus. Invite God into your heart and live according to His commandments. When you do, you will be blessed today, tomorrow, and forever.

SIX STEPS FOR DEALING WITH YOUR EMOTIONS

Accept the fact that emotions are powerful and that negative emotions are dangerous. God wants you to guard your heart against negative emotions and the destructive behaviors that negative emotions cause.

Recognize the fact that it's possible to control your emotions. It may take training and practice, but if you sincerely want to gain better control over your emotions, you can do it. With God, all things are possible.

Understand that emotions are contagious. Unless you make the conscious effort to take control of your thoughts and emotions, other people's emotions can hijack yours.

Identify any chronic negative feelings and turn them over to God. Make no room in your heart for bitterness, anger, regret, hatred, or any other negative emotion that threatens your sanity and robs you of peace.

When you experience a significant loss, express your feelings honestly. Express your grief. God promises to heal the broken-hearted. In time, He will dry your tears if you let Him. And, if you haven't already allowed Him to begin His healing process, today is perfect day to start.

Forgive everybody. It's God's rule, and it should be your rule too. The sooner you forgive, the sooner you'll feel better about yourself and your world.

1

THE QUESTION

Sometimes, especially when I'm tired, frustrated, or afraid, my emotions seem to go haywire. Why does this always seem to happen to me?

THE ANSWER

Emotions are contagious. When we're around people who are emotionally distraught, we're tempted to become upset too (unless we maintain a safe psychological distance from the emotional outburst). Also, our minds are like gardens. If we tend them with good thoughts, we reap a bountiful harvest. But if we allow them to be overgrown with negative thoughts, we reap a bitter harvest instead.

These things I have spoken to you, that in Me you may have peace. In the world you will have tribulation; but be of good cheer, I have overcome the world.

JOHN 16:33 NKJV

THE COST OF
NEGATIVE EMOTIONS

*Grow a wise heart—you'll do yourself a favor;
keep a clear head—you'll find a good life.*
PROVERBS 19:8 MSG

Time and again, the Bible instructs us to live by faith. Yet, despite our best intentions, negative feelings can rob us of the peace and abundance that could be ours—and should be ours—through Christ. When anger, frustration, impatience, or anxiety separates us from the spiritual blessings that God has in store, we must rethink our priorities. And we must place faith above feelings.

Human emotions are highly variable, decidedly unpredictable, and often unreliable. Our emotions change like the weather, but they're less predictable and far more fickle. So we must learn to live by faith, not by the ups and downs of our own emotional roller coasters.

Who's pulling your emotional strings? Are you allowing highly emotional people or highly charged situations to dictate your moods, or are you wiser than that? Sometime during the coming day, you may encounter a tough situation or a difficult person. And as a result, you may be gripped by a strong negative emotion. Distrust it. Reign it in. Test it. And turn it over to God.

Your emotions will inevitably change; God will not. So trust Him completely. When you do, you'll be surprised at how quickly those negative feelings will evaporate into thin air.

MORE FROM GOD'S WORD

All bitterness, anger and wrath, shouting and slander must be removed from you, along with all malice. And be kind and compassionate to one another, forgiving one another, just as God also forgave you in Christ.
EPHESIANS 4:31-32 HCSB

And let the peace of God rule in your hearts, to which also you were called in one body; and be thankful.
COLOSSIANS 3:15 NKJV

Get wisdom—how much better it is than gold! And get understanding—it is preferable to silver.
PROVERBS 16:16 HCSB

Enthusiasm without knowledge is not good. If you act too quickly, you might make a mistake.
PROVERBS 19:2 NCV

For this very reason, make every effort to supplement your faith with goodness, goodness with knowledge, knowledge with self-control, self-control with endurance, endurance with godliness.
2 PETER 1:5-6 HCSB

MORE THOUGHTS ABOUT EMOTIONS

A life lived in God is not lived on the plane of feelings, but of the will.

ELISABETH ELLIOT

It is Christ who is to be exalted, not our feelings. We will know Him by obedience, not by emotions. Our love will be shown by obedience, not by how good we feel about God at a given moment.

ELISABETH ELLIOT

Our emotions can lie to us, and we need to counter our emotions with truth.

BILLY GRAHAM

Our feelings do not affect God's facts.

AMY CARMICHAEL

Feelings are like chemicals; the more you analyze them the worse they smell.

CHARLES KINGSLEY

REMEMBER THIS

Human emotions are highly contagious, so when you're around people who are upset, you're more likely to become upset too. But if you're mentally prepared, you can resist negative emotions by making a conscious effort to stay calm.

GET PRACTICAL

The next time you encounter a difficult situation, be aware of your emotions. If you begin to get upset, worried, frustrated, or angry, catch yourself, take a deep breath, and calm yourself down. Don't allow other people's negative emotions to become your negative emotions.

A CONVERSATION STARTER

Talk to a friend about ways you both can stay calm when the people around you are upset or angry or both.

NOTES TO YOURSELF
ABOUT EMOTIONS

Write down your thoughts about the power of positive and negative emotions.

2

THE QUESTION

I try to be a disciplined person, but sometimes
I find it very hard to control my emotions.
What does the Bible say about that?

THE ANSWER

Throughout the Bible, we are taught that God
rewards self-discipline just as surely as He inevitably
punishes undisciplined behavior. Self-discipline
gives you more control. The more disciplined you
become, the more you can take control over your
emotions (which, by the way, is far better than
letting your emotions take control over you).

*God will give us the strength and resources
we need to live through any situation
in life that He ordains.*

BILLY GRAHAM

DISCIPLINE YOURSELF

Discipline yourself for the purpose of godliness.
1 TIMOTHY 4:7 NASB

When you find yourself caught up in an emotionally charged situation, it takes self-discipline to control yourself, but control yourself you must. Otherwise, you may find yourself caught up in an emotional outburst that results in bitter consequences.

God does not reward undisciplined behavior nor does He endorse impulsive outbursts. Instead, He instructs us to be mature, thoughtful, peaceful, and patient. Yet these qualities may not come naturally for most of us, so we need His help. When we petition Him in prayer, sincerely and often, He helps us reel in the negative emotions that, left unchecked, rob us of happiness and peace.

Life is a series of choices. Each day, we make countless decisions that can bring us closer to God or not. When we live according to the principles contained in God's Holy Word, we embark upon a journey of spiritual maturity that results in life abundant and life eternal.

Life's greatest rewards are seldom the result of luck. More often than not, our greatest accomplishments require plenty of preparation and lots of prayer, which is perfectly fine with God. After all, He knows that we can do the work, and He knows the rewards that we'll earn when we finish the job. Besides, God knows that He will always help us complete the tasks He has set before us. As a matter of fact, God usually does at least half the work: the second half. So if you're sincere about learning to control your emotions, make God your partner, and ask for His help. When you do, you can be sure that you and He, working together, can accomplish so much more than you can ever achieve by yourself.

MORE FROM GOD'S WORD

*Whatever you do, do your work heartily,
as for the Lord rather than for men.*
COLOSSIANS 3:23 NASB

*Better to be patient than powerful; better to
have self-control than to conquer a city.*
PROVERBS 16:32 NLT

*But the fruit of the Spirit is love, joy, peace,
patience, kindness, goodness, faith, gentleness,
self-control. Against such things there is no law.*
GALATIANS 5:22-23 HCSB

*Finishing is better than starting.
Patience is better than pride.*
ECCLESIASTES 7:8 NLT

*A final word: Be strong in the Lord
and in his mighty power.*
EPHESIANS 6:10 NLT

MORE THOUGHTS ABOUT SELF-DISCIPLINE

Personal discipline is a most powerful character quality and one worthy of dedicating your life to nurturing.

ELIZABETH GEORGE

No horse gets anywhere until he is harnessed. No stream or gas drives anything until it is confined. No life ever grows great until it is focused, dedicated, disciplined.

HARRY EMERSON FOSDICK

Being forced to work, and forced to do your best, will breed in you temperance and self-control, diligence and strength of will, cheerfulness and content, and a hundred virtues which the idle will never know.

CHARLES KINGSLEY

Think of something you ought to do and go do it. Heed not your feelings. Do your work.

GEORGE MacDONALD

Discipleship usually brings us into the necessity of choice between duty and desire.

ELISABETH ELLIOT

REMEMBER THIS

A disciplined lifestyle gives you more control: The more disciplined you become, the more you can take control over your emotions and your life (which, by the way, is far better than letting your emotions take control over you).

GET PRACTICAL

If you're a disciplined person, you'll earn big rewards. If you're undisciplined, you won't. Act accordingly.

—⁓—

A CONVERSATION STARTER

Talk to a friend about tangible steps you can take to lead a more disciplined life.

NOTES TO YOURSELF
ABOUT SELF-DISCIPLINE

Write down your thoughts about the rewards of self-discipline and the dangers of undisciplined behaviors.

3

THE QUESTION

How does my behavior impact
my emotional health?

THE ANSWER

When we obey God and live in accordance with
His teachings, we feel better about ourselves.
But when we stray from His path, we inevitably
create negative emotions like guilt, worry, or
shame. Obedience enhances emotional health;
disobedience doesn't.

*Our battles are first won or lost in the secret
places of our will in God's presence,
never in full view of the world.*

OSWALD CHAMBERS

DOING THE RIGHT THING

Now by this we know that we know Him,
if we keep His commandments.

1 JOHN 2:3 NKJV

God's instructions to mankind are contained in a book like no other: the Holy Bible. When we obey God's commandments and listen carefully to the conscience He has placed in our hearts, we are secure. But if we disobey our Creator, if we choose to ignore the teachings and the warnings of His Word, we do so at great peril.

Susanna Wesley said, "There are two things to do about the Gospel: believe it and behave it." Her words serve as a powerful reminder that, as Christians, we are called to take God's promises seriously and to live in accordance with His teachings.

God gave us His commandments for a reason: so that we might obey them and be blessed. Yet we live in a world that presents us with countless temptations to stray far from His path. It is our responsibility to resist those temptations with vigor. Obedience isn't just the best way to experience the full measure of God's blessings; it's the only way.

MORE FROM GOD'S WORD

In everything set them an example
by doing what is good.
Titus 2:7 NIV

But prove yourselves doers of the word, and not
merely hearers who delude themselves.
James 1:22 NASB

To do evil is like sport to a fool, but a man of
understanding has wisdom.
Proverbs 10:23 NKJV

Live peaceful and quiet lives in
all godliness and holiness.
1 Timothy 2:2 NIV

Walk in a manner worthy of the God who
calls you into His own kingdom and glory.
1 Thessalonians 2:12 NASB

MORE THOUGHTS ABOUT BEHAVIOR

One of the real tests of Christian character is to be found in the lives we live from day to day.

BILLY GRAHAM

If we judge our conduct by Christ and his desire to please the Father, we will solve many decisions regarding behavior.

ERWIN LUTZER

Our walk counts far more than our talk, always!

GEORGE MUELLER

Never support an experience which does not have God as its source and faith in God as its result.

OSWALD CHAMBERS

God is voting for us all the time. The devil is voting against us all the time. The way we vote carries the election.

CORRIE TEN BOOM

MORE THOUGHTS ABOUT BEHAVIOR

REMEMBER THIS

Try as we might, we simply cannot escape the consequences of our actions. How we behave today has a direct impact on the rewards we will receive tomorrow. Responsible behavior bears good fruit; bad behavior doesn't.

GET PRACTICAL

Ask yourself if your behavior has been radically changed by your unfolding relationship with God. If the answer is unclear to you—or if the answer is no—think of a single step you can take, a positive change, that will bring you closer to your Creator.

A CONVERSATION STARTER

Talk to a friend about ways to keep explosive emotions in check.

NOTES TO YOURSELF
ABOUT DOING THE RIGHT THING

Write down your thoughts about self-improvement. List a few behaviors you'd like to change.

4

THE QUESTION

Sometimes my emotions get the best of me,
and I act impulsively. What does the Bible
say about that?

THE ANSWER

God's Word warns against the dangers of
impulsive behavior. If you can't seem to put
the brakes on impulsive behavior,
you may not be praying hard enough.

Patience and encouragement...come from God.

ROMANS 15:5 NCV

SLOW DOWN!

Enthusiasm without knowledge is no good;
haste makes mistakes.
PROVERBS 19:2 NLT

When you encounter a person with a difficult personality, do you respond without thinking? Do you react first and think about your reaction second? Are you simply a little too hot-headed for your own good? If so, God's Word has some advice for you.

The Bible teaches us to be self-controlled, thoughtful, and mature. But the world often tempts us to behave otherwise. Everywhere we turn, or so it seems, we see undisciplined, unruly role models who behave impulsively yet experience few, if any, negative consequences. So it's not surprising that when we meet folks whose personalities conflict with our own, we're tempted to respond in undisciplined, unruly ways. But there's a catch: If we fall prey to immaturity or impulsivity, those behaviors inevitably cause us many more problems than they solve.

Our impulses may lead us astray, but our heavenly Father never will. So if you're wise, you'll learn to slow yourself down, take a deep breath, and consult God before you strike out in anger, not after.

MORE FROM GOD'S WORD

Don't let your spirit rush to be angry,
for anger abides in the heart of fools.
ECCLESIASTES 7:9 HCSB

Do you see a man who speaks too soon?
There is more hope for a fool than for him.
PROVERBS 29:20 HCSB

Those who guard their lips preserve their lives,
but those who speak rashly will come to ruin.
PROVERBS 13:3 NIV

A patient spirit is better than a proud spirit.
ECCLESIASTES 7:8 HCSB

A prudent person foresees danger
and takes precautions. The simpleton goes
blindly on and suffers the consequences.
PROVERBS 22:3 NLT

MORE THOUGHTS
ABOUT IMPULSIVITY

Zeal without knowledge is fire without light.

THOMAS FULLER

Patience is the companion of wisdom.

ST. AUGUSTINE

*In times of uncertainty, wait. Always, if you have
any doubt, wait. Do not force yourself to any
action. If you have a restraint in your spirit,
wait until all is clear, and do not go against it.*

LETTIE COWMAN

*We must learn to wait. There is grace
supplied to the one who waits.*

LETTIE COWMAN

*Nothing is more terrible than
activity without insight.*

THOMAS CARLYLE

REMEMBER THIS

If you're a little too emotional or a little too impulsive, it's time to begin a serious dialogue with God. He wants you to behave wisely, not impulsively. Your intentions should be the same.

GET PRACTICAL

If you can't seem to put the brakes on impulsive behavior, you're not praying hard enough. Ask God to help you slow down, to think before you act, and to look before you leap.

―⁂―

A CONVERSATION STARTER

Talk to a friend about the dangers of emotional decisions and impulsive actions.

NOTES TO YOURSELF
ABOUT IMPULSIVITY

Write down your thoughts about the dangers of impulsive behavior.

_____

_____

_____

_____

_____

_____

_____

_____

_____

_____

5

THE QUESTION

When people upset me, my emotions seem to take over. What can I do to control my emotions?

THE ANSWER

One thing you can do is to pray early and often about the people who have upset you. It's a great way to make sure your heart is in tune with God. The more you talk to Him, the more He will talk to you.

A feeling of real need is always a good enough reason to pray.

HANNAH WHITALL SMITH

SILENT PRAYERS TO THE RESCUE

I desire therefore that the men pray everywhere,
lifting up holy hands, without wrath and doubting.
1 Timothy 2:8 NKJV

If you're having trouble dealing with your emotions, talk to God about it. The Lord has many important lessons to teach you, and this may be one of them. He has promised to guide you and protect you. Your task, simply put, is to listen and obey.

Perhaps, on occasion, you may find yourself overwhelmed by the challenges of everyday life. Perhaps you may forget to slow yourself down long enough to talk with God about the matters that concern you. Instead of turning your thoughts and prayers to Him, you may rely upon your own resources. Instead of asking God for guidance, you may depend only upon your own limited wisdom. A far better course of action is this: Stop what you're doing long enough to open your heart to the Creator; then listen carefully for His directions. In all things great and small, seek the Lord's wisdom and His grace. He hears your prayers, and He will answer. All you must do is ask.

MORE FROM GOD'S WORD

*Ask, and it will be given to you; seek, and you
will find; knock, and it will be opened to you.
For everyone who asks receives, and he who seeks
finds, and to him who knocks it will be opened.*
Matthew 7:7-8 NASB

*Confess your trespasses to one another,
and pray for one another, that you may be healed.
The effective, fervent prayer of a righteous man
avails much.*
James 5:16 NKJV

*And whenever you stand praying,
if you have anything against anyone, forgive him,
so that your Father in heaven may also
forgive you your wrongdoing.*
Mark 11:25 HCSB

Is anyone among you suffering? He should pray.
James 5:13 HCSB

*Rejoice always, pray without ceasing,
in everything give thanks; for this is the will
of God in Christ Jesus for you.*
1 Thessalonians 5:16-18 NKJV

MORE THOUGHTS ABOUT PRAYER

Two wings are necessary to lift our souls toward God: prayer and praise. Prayer asks. Praise accepts the answer.

LETTIE COWMAN

Any concern that is too small to be turned into a prayer is too small to be made into a burden.

CORRIE TEN BOOM

It is impossible to overstate the need for prayer in the fabric of family life.

JAMES DOBSON

Prayer is our lifeline to God.

BILLY GRAHAM

Don't pray when you feel like it. Have an appointment with the Lord and keep it.

CORRIE TEN BOOM

REMEMBER THIS

If you're having trouble dealing with a difficult person, pray about it. Prayer changes things, and it changes you. So pray.

GET PRACTICAL

If you're having trouble with another person, pray for that person and pray for guidance. When you ask for God's help, He'll heal your heart and guide your path.

—⁂—

A CONVERSATION STARTER

Talk to a friend about your experiences concerning prayer: times when your prayer life was meaningful, and times when you found it hard to pray. How did the quality and quantity of your prayers impact the other aspects of your life?

NOTES TO YOURSELF
ABOUT PRAYER

Write down your thoughts about the power of prayer.

6

THE QUESTION

Sometimes it's easy for me to become angry.
What does the Bible say about anger?

THE ANSWER

The Bible warns us time and again about anger.
So the next time you're confronted by a difficult
person and you're tempted to lose your cool,
walk away before you get carried away.

*We must meet our disappointments,
our malicious enemies, our provoking friends,
our trials of every sort, with an attitude of
surrender and trust. We must rise above them
in Christ so they lose their power to harm us.*

Hannah Whitall Smith

BEYOND ANGER

*Do not let the sun go down on your anger,
and do not give the devil an opportunity.*
EPHESIANS 4:26-27 NASB

Anger is harmful, hurtful, and dangerous to your spiritual health. Whenever your thoughts are hijacked by angry emotions, you forfeit the peace and perspective that might otherwise be yours. And to make matters worse, angry thoughts can cause you to behave in irrational, self-destructive ways. As the old saying goes, "Anger is only one letter away from danger."

1 Peter 5:8-9 warns, "Stay alert! Watch out for your great enemy, the devil. He prowls around like a roaring lion, looking for someone to devour. Stand firm against him, and be strong in your faith." (NLT).

And of this you can be sure: Your adversary will use an unforgiving heart, and the inevitable anger that dwells within it, to sabotage your life and undermine your faith. To be safe, you must cleanse your heart, and you must forgive. You must say yes to God, yes to mercy, yes to love, and no to anger.

MORE FROM GOD'S WORD

*Everyone must be quick to hear, slow to speak,
and slow to anger, for man's anger does not
accomplish God's righteousness.*
JAMES 1:19-20 HCSB

*A hot-tempered man stirs up conflict,
but a man slow to anger calms strife.*
PROVERBS 15:18 HCSB

*But now you must also put away all the following:
anger, wrath, malice, slander,
and filthy language from your mouth.*
COLOSSIANS 3:8 HCSB

*He who is slow to wrath has great understanding,
but he who is impulsive exalts folly.*
PROVERBS 14:29 NKJV

*But I tell you that anyone who is angry with a
brother or sister will be subject to judgment.*
MATTHEW 5:22 NIV

MORE THOUGHTS
ABOUT ANGER

Frustration is not the will of God. There is time to do anything and everything that God wants us to do.

ELISABETH ELLIOT

Life is too short to spend it being angry, bored, or dull.

BARBARA JOHNSON

Hence it is not enough to deal with the Temper. We must go to the source, and change the inmost nature, and the angry humors will die away of themselves.

HENRY DRUMMOND

Hot heads and cold hearts never solved anything.

BILLY GRAHAM

Anger and bitterness—whatever the cause—only end up hurting us. Turn that anger over to Christ.

BILLY GRAHAM

REMEMBER THIS

Emotions are highly contagious and angry encounters almost never have happy endings. So if someone is ranting, raving, or worse, you have the right to leave the scene of the argument.

GET PRACTICAL

If you think you're about to explode in anger, slow down, take a deep breath, and walk away from the scene of the argument. It's better to walk away—and keep walking—than it is to blurt out angry words that can't be un-blurted.

—⁓—

A CONVERSATION STARTER

Talk to a friend about the consequences of angry outbursts. How do they impact others? How do they impact your own emotional health?

NOTES TO YOURSELF
ABOUT ANGER

Write down your thoughts about the costs and the dangers of angry outbursts. What are better ways to respond?

7

THE QUESTION

I've experienced a significant loss, and it
feels like my grieving will never end.
What does the Bible say about that?

THE ANSWER

God promises to heal the brokenhearted. In time,
He will dry your tears if you let Him. And if you
haven't already allowed Him to begin His healing
process, today is the perfect day to start.

*Fold the arms of your faith and wait in quietness
until the light goes up in your darkness.*

GEORGE MACDONALD

GOD'S ANSWER TO GRIEF

Blessed are the poor in spirit: for theirs is the kingdom of heaven. Blessed are they that mourn: for they shall be comforted.

MATTHEW 5:3-4 KJV

Every significant loss carries with it significant pain, but grieving Christians find strength and comfort in their faith. When we talk to God—and listen carefully for His response—He offers assurance, courage, strength, and renewal. So during times of intense grief, wise Christians renew themselves through prayer, through worship, and through a careful study of God's Holy Word.

Grief visits all of us who live long and love deeply. When we lose a loved one, or when we experience any other profound loss, darkness overwhelms us for a while, and it seems as if our purpose for living has vanished. Thankfully, God has other plans.

The Christian faith, as communicated through the words of the Holy Bible, is a healing faith. It offers comfort in times of trouble, courage for our fears, hope instead of hopelessness. For Christians, the grave is not a final resting place; it is a place of transition. Through the healing words of God's promises, Christians understand that the Lord continues to manifest His plan in good times and bad.

If you are experiencing the intense pain of a recent loss, or if you are still mourning a loss from long ago, perhaps you are now ready to begin the next stage of your journey with God. If so, be mindful of this fact: As a wounded survivor, you will have countless opportunities to serve others. And by serving others, you will bring purpose and meaning to the suffering you've endured.

MORE FROM GOD'S WORD

Weeping may endure for a night,
but joy cometh in the morning.
PSALM 30:5 KJV

Ye shall be sorrowful, but your sorrow
shall be turned into joy.
JOHN 16:20 KJV

The LORD shall give thee rest from thy sorrow,
and from thy fear.
ISAIAH 14:3 KJV

He heals the brokenhearted
and binds up their wounds.
PSALM 147:3 HCSB

The LORD is near to those
who have a broken heart.
PSALM 34:18 NKJV

MORE THOUGHTS
ABOUT GRIEF

Despair is always the gateway of faith.

OSWALD CHAMBERS

*God is sufficient for all our needs,
for every problem, for every difficulty,
for every broken heart, for every human sorrow.*

PETER MARSHALL

*Your greatest ministry will most likely
come out of your greatest hurt.*

RICK WARREN

*If there is something we need more than anything
else during grief, it is a friend who stands with us,
who doesn't leave us. Jesus is that friend.*

BILLY GRAHAM

*God has enough grace to solve every
dilemma you face, wipe every tear you cry,
and answer every question you ask.*

MAX LUCADO

REMEMBER THIS

Grief is a universal fact of life; no man or woman, no matter how righteous, is exempt. Christians, however, face their grief with the ultimate armor: God's promises. God will help heal us if we let Him into our hearts. And the time to let Him in is now.

GET PRACTICAL

Grief is not meant to be avoided or feared; it is meant to be worked through. Grief hurts, but denying your true feelings can hurt even more. With God's help, you can face your pain and move beyond it.

—⁓—

A CONVERSATION STARTER

If you're grieving, don't keep your emotions bottled up inside. Find someone you can trust and talk about it.

NOTES TO YOURSELF
ABOUT EXPRESSING GRIEF

Write down your thoughts about the need to express your grief and the costs of not expressing it.

8

THE QUESTION

It seems like I'm always beating myself up over something I've done wrong. If I feel guilty about something, what should I do?

THE ANSWER

First, be certain that you're no longer doing the thing that caused your guilt in the first place. Then ask for forgiveness (from God and from anybody you've hurt). Next, make sure to forgive yourself. And finally, if you still have residual feelings of bitterness or regret, keep asking God to heal your heart. When you ask, He will answer in His own time and in His own way.

———※———

The purpose of guilt is to bring us to Jesus. Once we are there, then its purpose is finished. If we continue to make ourselves guilty— to blame ourselves—then that is a sin in itself.

CORRIE TEN BOOM

BEYOND GUILT

Blessed are those who don't feel guilty for doing something they have decided is right.

ROMANS 14:22 NLT

All of us have sinned. We've all made countless mistakes and fallen short of the mark on too many occasions to count. Sometimes our sins result from our own stubborn rebellion against God's commandments. And sometimes, we are swept up in events that are beyond our abilities to control. Under either set of circumstances, we may experience intense feelings of guilt. But God has an answer for the guilt that we feel. That answer, of course, is His forgiveness.

When we confess our wrongdoings and repent from them, we are forgiven by the One who created us. Genuine repentance requires more than simply offering God apologies for our misdeeds. Real repentance may start with feelings of sorrow and remorse, but it ends only when we turn away from the sin that has heretofore distanced us from our Creator. In truth, we offer our most meaningful apologies to God, not with our words, but with our actions. As long as we are still engaged in sin, we may be "repenting," but we have not fully "repented."

Are you troubled by feelings of guilt or regret? If so, you must first repent from your misdeeds, and you must ask your heavenly Father for His forgiveness. When you do so, He will forgive you completely and without reservation. Then you must forgive yourself just as God has forgiven you: thoroughly, unconditionally, and eternally.

MORE FROM GOD'S WORD

Be gracious to me, God, according to Your faithful
love; according to Your abundant compassion,
blot out my rebellion. Wash away my guilt,
and cleanse me from my sin.
PSALM 51:1-2 HCSB

Let us come near to God with a sincere heart and
a sure faith, because we have been made free
from a guilty conscience, and our bodies have
been washed with pure water.
HEBREWS 10:22 NCV

How can I know all the sins lurking in my heart?
Cleanse me from these hidden faults.
Keep your servant from deliberate sins!
Don't let them control me. Then I will be free
of guilt and innocent of great sin.
PSALM 19:12-13 NLT

Create in me a pure heart, God,
and make my spirit right again.
PSALM 51:10 NCV

Consider my affliction and rescue me,
for I have not forgotten Your instruction.
PSALM 119:153 HCSB

MORE THOUGHTS ABOUT GUILT

The redemption, accomplished for us by our Lord Jesus Christ on the cross at Calvary, is redemption from the power of sin as well as from its guilt. Christ is able to save all who come unto God by Him.

HANNAH WHITALL SMITH

Guilt is an appalling waste of energy; you can't build on it. It's only good for wallowing in.

KATHERINE MANSFIELD

The most marvelous ingredient in the forgiveness of God is that he also forgets, the one thing a human being cannot do. With God, forgetting is a divine attribute. God's forgiveness forgets.

OSWALD CHAMBERS

God's mercy is boundless, free, and, through Jesus Christ our Lord, available to us in our present situation.

A. W. TOZER

God does not wish us to remember what he is willing to forget.

GEORGE A. BUTTRICK

REMEMBER THIS

Guilt is God's warning system. So if you feel guilty about something, you can be sure that God wants you to stop doing it right now. Then, when you've put an end to the bad behavior and asked for God's forgiveness, He wipes the slate clean.

GET PRACTICAL

If you've asked for God's forgiveness, He has given it. But have you forgiven yourself? If not, the very best moment to do so is the present moment.

—⚬⚬⚬—

A CONVERSATION STARTER

Talk to a friend about God's forgiveness and how we should react when He forgives and forgets our sins.

NOTES TO YOURSELF ABOUT GUILT

Write down your thoughts about the futility of guilt and the dangers of ignoring God's forgiveness.

NOTES TO MYSELF ABOUT LIFE

9

THE QUESTION

I'm an adult, but I've still got so much to learn.
What should I do?

THE ANSWER

Whether you're a young adult or a seasoned
senior citizen, you can still learn better strategies
for dealing with the ups and downs of life. God
doesn't intend for you to be a stagnant Christian.
So, you should never stop learning.

*Keep asking, and it will be given to you. Keep
searching, and you will find. Keep knocking, and
the door will be opened to you. For everyone who
asks receives, and the one who searches finds, and
to the one who knocks, the door will be opened.*

MATTHEW 7:7-8 HCSB

KEEP LEARNING

Wisdom is the principal thing; therefore get wisdom.
And in all your getting, get understanding.

PROVERBS 4:7 NKJV

Learning to control your emotions is a process. It takes time, patience, and prayer. And with God's help, you can do it.

The Bible makes this promise: If we genuinely desire wisdom, and if we're willing to search for it, we will find it. And where should the search begin? The answer, of course, is in God's Holy Word.

The search for wisdom should be a lifelong journey, not a destination. We should continue to read, to watch, and to learn new things as long as we live. But it's not enough to learn new things or to memorize the great biblical truths; we must also live by them.

So, what will you learn today? Will you take time feed your mind and fill your heart? And will you study the guidebook that God has given you? Hopefully so, because His plans and His promises are waiting for you there, inside the covers of a book like no other: His Book. It contains the essential wisdom you'll need to navigate the seas of life and land safely on that distant shore.

MORE FROM GOD'S WORD

Commit yourself to instruction;
listen carefully to words of knowledge.
PROVERBS 23:12 NLT

Enthusiasm without knowledge is not good. If you
act too quickly, you might make a mistake.
PROVERBS 19:2 NCV

Joyful is the person who finds wisdom,
the one who gains understanding.
PROVERBS 3:13 NLT

Teach me Your way, Yahweh, and I will
live by Your truth. Give me an undivided mind
to fear Your name.
PSALM 86:11 HCSB

Anyone who listens to my teaching
and follows it is wise, like a person
who builds a house on solid rock.
MATTHEW 7:24 NLT

MORE THOUGHTS
ABOUT LIFETIME LEARNING

Life is not a holiday but an education. And, the one eternal lesson for all of us is how we can love.

HENRY DRUMMOND

True learning can take place at every age of life, and it doesn't have to be in the curriculum plan.

SUZANNE DALE EZELL

A time of trouble and darkness is meant to teach you lessons you desperately need.

LETTIE COWMAN

Every day we live is a priceless gift of God, loaded with possibilities to learn something new, to gain fresh insights.

DALE EVANS ROGERS

Learning makes a man fit company for himself.

THOMAS FULLER

REMEMBER THIS

You still have lots to learn about yourself. Sometimes, God allows us to endure difficult circumstances so that we might grow and mature as Christians.

GET PRACTICAL

Make it a point to study God's Word every day. When you do, you'll become a better person and a better Christian.

—◈—

A CONVERSATION STARTER

Talk to a friend about ways that you both have matured during the last few years. Have tough times taught you lessons you couldn't have learned any other way?

NOTES TO YOURSELF
ABOUT LIFETIME LEARNING

Write down your thoughts about the joys and the rewards of lifetime learning.

10

THE QUESTION

Sometimes I'm overly anxious, and sometimes I'm more fearful than I should be. What does the Bible say about fear?

THE ANSWER

If you're feeling fearful or anxious, you must trust God to handle the problems that are simply too big for you to solve.

Meet your fears with faith.

MAX LUCADO

FACING FEARS

Fear not, for I am with you; Be not dismayed, for I am your God. I will strengthen you, Yes, I will help you, I will uphold you with My righteous right hand.

Isaiah 41:10 NKJV

From time to time, all of us experience difficult days when unexpected circumstances test our mettle. When these situations occur, fear creeps in and threatens to overtake our minds and our hearts.

Difficult times call for courageous measures. Running away from problems only perpetuates them; fear begets more fear; and anxiety is a poor counselor.

Adversity visits everyone—no human being is beyond Old Man Trouble's reach. But, Old Man Trouble is not only an unwelcome guest, he is also an invaluable teacher. If we are to become mature human beings, it is our duty to learn from the inevitable hardships and heartbreaks of life.

Today, ask God to help you step beyond the boundaries of your fear. Ask Him to guide you to a place where you can realize your potential—a place where you are freed from the paralysis of anxiety. Ask Him to do His part, and then promise Him that you'll do your part. Don't ask God to lead you to a safe place; ask Him to lead you to the right place. And remember that those two places are seldom the same.

MORE FROM GOD'S WORD

Be not afraid, only believe.
Mark 5:36 KJV

*The Lord is my light and my salvation—whom
should I fear? The Lord is the stronghold of my life—
of whom should I be afraid?*
Psalm 27:1 HCSB

*Even though I walk through the darkest valley,
I will fear no evil, for you are with me;
your rod and your staff, they comfort me.*
Psalm 23:4 NIV

*Peace I leave with you; My peace I give to you;
not as the world gives do I give to you. Do not let
your heart be troubled, nor let it be fearful.*
John 14:27 NASB

But He said to them, "It is I; do not be afraid."
John 6:20 NKJV

MORE THOUGHTS
ABOUT FEAR

*It is good to remind ourselves that the will of God
comes from the heart of God and that
we need not be afraid.*

WARREN WIERSBE

*The Lord Jesus by His Holy Spirit is with me,
and the knowledge of His presence dispels
the darkness and allays any fears.*

BILL BRIGHT

A perfect faith would lift us absolutely above fear.

GEORGE MACDONALD

*The presence of fear does not mean you
have no faith. Fear visits everyone. But make
your fear a visitor and not a resident.*

MAX LUCADO

*Only believe, don't fear. Our Master, Jesus,
always watches over us, and no matter what
the persecution, Jesus will surely overcome it.*

LOTTIE MOON

REMEMBER THIS

If you're feeling fearful or anxious, you must trust God to solve the problems that are simply too big for you to solve on your own.

GET PRACTICAL

Are you feeling anxious or fearful? If so, trust God to handle those problems that are simply too big for you to solve. Entrust the future—your future—to God. The two of you, working together, can accomplish great things for His kingdom.

—w—

A CONVERSATION STARTER

Talk to a friend about the kinds of fears that may be holding you back.

NOTES TO YOURSELF
ABOUT FEAR

Write down your thoughts about the role that fear plays in your life. Are you too fearful? Or not fearful enough?

11

THE QUESTION

When I'm overcome by anxiety and worries, what should I do? And where should I turn?

THE ANSWER

Carefully divide your areas of concern into two categories: those things you can control and those you cannot control. Once you've done so, spend your time working to resolve the things you can control, and entrust everything else to God.

Claim all of God's promises in the Bible.
Your sins, your worries, your life—
you may cast them all on Him.

CORRIE TEN BOOM

BEYOND THE ANXIETIES

*Therefore do not worry about tomorrow,
for tomorrow will worry about its own things.
Sufficient for the day is its own trouble.*

MATTHEW 6:34 NKJV

Because we are human beings who have the capacity to think and to anticipate future events, we worry. We worry about big things, little things, and just about everything in between. To make matters worse, we live in a world that breeds anxiety and fosters fear. So it's not surprising that when we come face to face with tough times, we may fall prey to discouragement, doubt, or depression. But our Father in heaven has other plans.

God has promised that we may lead lives of abundance, not anxiety. In fact, His Word instructs us to "be anxious for nothing." But how can we put our fears to rest? By taking those fears to Him and leaving them there.

The very same God who created the universe has promised to protect you now and forever. So what do you have to worry about? With God on your side, the answer is, nothing.

MORE FROM GOD'S WORD

*Cast your burden on the L*ORD*, And He
shall sustain you; He shall never permit
the righteous to be moved.*

PSALM 55:22 NKJV

*Peace I leave with you; My peace I give to you;
not as the world gives do I give to you. Do not let
your heart be troubled, nor let it be fearful.*

JOHN 14:27 NASB

*Do not be anxious about anything, but in every
situation, by prayer and petition, with thanksgiving,
present your requests to God.*

PHILIPPIANS 4:6 NIV

*Cast all your anxiety on him
because he cares for you.*

1 PETER 5:7 NIV

*Let not your heart be troubled;
you believe in God, believe also in Me.*

JOHN 14:1 NKJV

MORE THOUGHTS ABOUT ANXIETY

Tomorrow is busy worrying about itself;
don't get tangled up in its worry-webs.

SARAH YOUNG

Do not worry about tomorrow.
This is not a suggestion, but a command.

SARAH YOUNG

Anxiety and fear are like baby tigers. The more
you feed them, the stronger they grow.

BILLY GRAHAM

Worry is the senseless process of
cluttering up tomorrow's opportunities
with leftover problems from today.

BARBARA JOHNSON

Pray, and let God worry.

MARTIN LUTHER

REMEMBER THIS

You have worries, but God has solutions. Your challenge is to trust Him to solve the problems that are simply too big for you to resolve on your own.

GET PRACTICAL

Divide your areas of concern into two categories: those you can control and those you can't. Focus on the former and refuse to waste time or energy worrying about the latter.

—⁓—

A CONVERSATION STARTER

Talk to a friend about ways to trust God more and worry less.

NOTES TO YOURSELF
ABOUT ANXIETIES

Make a list of the worries that you should turn over to God right now. Then, pray about your list.

....

....

....

....

....

....

....

....

....

....

12

THE QUESTION

Sometimes, I'm tempted to gripe and complain about the difficult people in my life. What does the Bible say about complaining?

THE ANSWER

God's Word teaches us that perpetual complaining is a very bad habit. And it's contagious. So please be sure that your friends and family members don't catch it from you!

No matter what our circumstance,
we can find a reason to be thankful.

DAVID JEREMIAH

THE FUTILITY
OF COMPLAINING

Be hospitable to one another without complaining.
1 PETER 4:9 HCSB

Most of us have more blessings than we can count, yet we still find things to complain about. To complain, of course, is not only shortsighted, but it is also a serious roadblock on the path to spiritual abundance. Yet in our weakest moments we still grumble, whine, and moan about difficult people or the difficult circumstances they seem to create on a daily basis. Sometimes we give voice to our complaints, and on other occasions, we manage to keep our protestations to ourselves. But even when no one else hears our complaints, God does.

Would you like to feel more comfortable about your circumstances and your life? Then promise yourself that you'll do whatever it takes to ensure that you focus your thoughts and energy on the major blessings you've received, not the minor hardships—or the difficult people—you must occasionally endure.

So the next time you're tempted to complain about the inevitable frustrations of everyday living, don't do it. Today and every day, make it a practice to count your blessings, not your inconveniences. It's the truly decent way to live.

MORE FROM GOD'S WORD

*My dear brothers and sisters, always be
willing to listen and slow to speak.*
JAMES 1:19 NCV

*A fool's displeasure is known at once,
but whoever ignores an insult is sensible.*
PROVERBS 12:16 HCSB

*Those who consider themselves religious
and yet do not keep a tight rein on their tongues
deceive themselves, and their religion is worthless.*
JAMES 1:26 NIV

*Those who guard their lips guards their lives,
but those who speak rashly will come to ruin.*
PROVERBS 13:3 NIV

*Do everything without complaining or arguing.
Then you will be innocent and without any wrong.*
PHILIPPIANS 2:14-15 NCV

MORE THOUGHTS
ABOUT COMPLAINING

*It is always possible to be thankful for what is given
rather than to complain about what is not given.
One or the other becomes a habit of life.*

ELISABETH ELLIOT

*If we have our eyes upon ourselves, our problems,
and our pain, we cannot lift our eyes upward.*

BILLY GRAHAM

*Grumbling and gratitude are, for the child of God,
in conflict. Be grateful and you won't grumble.
Grumble and you won't be grateful.*

BILLY GRAHAM

*Thanksgiving or complaining—these words express
two contrasting attitudes of the souls of God's
children. The soul that gives thanks can find
comfort in everything; the soul that complains
can find comfort in nothing.*

HANNAH WHITALL SMITH

*Don't complain. The more you complain
about things, the more things you'll have
to complain about.*

E. STANLEY JONES

REMEMBER THIS

If you genuinely seek God's peace, you'll fill your heart with gratitude. When you do, there's simply no room left for complaints about tough times, unfortunate circumstances, or anything else for that matter.

GET PRACTICAL

Try to keep track of the times you complain, either to someone else or to yourself. Also, make note of the times you express gratitude to the Lord. Do you spend more time complaining or praising?

—w—

A CONVERSATION STARTER

Talk to a friend about the emotional and spiritual costs associated with constant complaining. And if you complain more than you should, talk about ways that you can shutter your personal complaint factory for good.

NOTES TO YOURSELF
ABOUT COMPLAINING

List ways you can complain less and do more.

13

THE QUESTION

Stressful situations upset me more than they should. What does the Bible say about my ability to experience God's peace?

THE ANSWER

God's peace surpasses human understanding, and it's available to all. When we accept His peace, it revolutionizes our lives.

Prayer guards hearts and minds and causes God to bring peace out of chaos.

BETH MOORE

PEACE IS POSSIBLE

Peace I leave with you, My peace I give to you;
not as the world gives do I give to you. Let not
your heart be troubled, neither let it be afraid.
JOHN 14:27 NKJV

Peace. It's such a beautiful word. It conveys images of serenity, contentment, and freedom from the trials and tribulations of everyday existence. Peace means freedom from conflict, freedom from inner turmoil, and freedom from worry. Peace is such a beautiful concept that advertisers and marketers attempt to sell it with images of relaxed vacationers lounging on the beach or happy senior citizens celebrating on the golf course. But contrary to the implied claims of modern media, real peace, genuine peace, isn't for sale. At any price.

Have you discovered the genuine peace that can be yours through Christ? Or are you still scurrying after the illusion of peace that the world promises but cannot deliver? If you've turned things over to Jesus, you'll be blessed now and forever. So what are you waiting for? Let Him rule your heart and your thoughts, beginning now. When you do, you'll experience the peace that only He can give.

MORE FROM GOD'S WORD

These things I have spoken to you,
that in Me you may have peace. In the world
you will have tribulation; but be of good cheer,
I have overcome the world.
JOHN 16:33 NKJV

But the fruit of the Spirit is love, joy, peace,
patience, kindness, goodness, faith, gentleness,
self-control. Against such things there is no law.
GALATIANS 5:22-23 HCSB

"I will give peace, real peace, to those far
and near, and I will heal them," says the LORD.
ISAIAH 57:19 NCV

The peace of God, which passeth all
understanding, shall keep your hearts
and minds through Christ Jesus.
PHILIPPIANS 4:7 KJV

He Himself is our peace.
EPHESIANS 2:14 NASB

MORE THOUGHTS ABOUT PEACE

*Peace does not mean to be in a place where
there is no noise, trouble, or hard work.
Peace means to be in the midst of all those things
and still be calm in your heart.*

CATHERINE MARSHALL

*Only Christ can meet the deepest needs
of our world and our hearts. Christ alone
can bring lasting peace.*

BILLY GRAHAM

*God's power is great enough for our
deepest desperation. You can go on.
You can pick up the pieces and start anew.
You can face your fears. You can find peace
in the rubble. There is healing for your soul.*

SUZANNE DALE EZELL

*Deep within the center of the soul is a chamber
of peace where God lives and where,
if we will enter it and quiet all the other sounds,
we can hear His gentle whisper.*

LETTIE COWMAN

*In the center of a hurricane there is absolute
quiet and peace. There is no safer place than in
the center of the will of God.*

CORRIE TEN BOOM

REMEMBER THIS

God's peace is available to you this very moment if you place absolute trust in Him. The Lord is your shepherd. Trust Him today and be blessed.

GET PRACTICAL

God's peace can be yours if you open up your heart and invite Him in. He can restore your soul if you let Him. The rest is up to you.

—⁂—

A CONVERSATION STARTER

The Lord promises that we can experience the peace that passes all understanding. Talk to a friend about ways both of you can discover God's peace.

NOTES TO YOURSELF
ABOUT PEACE

Write down your thoughts about finding peace and keeping it.

....

....

....

....

....

....

....

....

....

....

14

THE QUESTION

I can talk to God, but I have trouble waiting for His answers. What does the Bible say about listening to God?

THE ANSWER

Whether you are communicating with God or with other people, it's always a good idea to listen more than you talk.

The purpose of all prayer is to find God's will and to make that our prayer.

CATHERINE MARSHALL

LISTEN

Be still, and know that I am God.
PSALM 46:10 KJV

God speaks to us in different ways at different times. Sometimes He speaks loudly and clearly. But more often, He speaks in a quiet voice—and if you are wise, you will be listening carefully when He does. To do so, you must carve out quiet moments each day to study His Word and to sense His direction.

Are you willing to pray sincerely and then wait quietly for God's response? Can you quiet yourself long enough to listen to your conscience? Are you attuned to the subtle guidance of your intuition? Hopefully so. Usually God refrains from sending His messages on stone tablets or city billboards. More often, He communicates in subtler ways. If you sincerely desire to hear His voice, you must listen carefully, and you must do so in the silent corners of your quiet, willing heart.

MORE FROM GOD'S WORD

Be silent before Me.
ISAIAH 41:1 HCSB

*Listen, listen to me, and eat what is good,
and you will delight in the richest of fare. Give ear
and come to me; listen, that you may live.*
ISAIAH 55:2-3 NIV

*The one who is from God listens to God's words.
This is why you don't listen, because you
are not from God.*
JOHN 8:47 HCSB

Rest in the LORD, and wait patiently for Him.
PSALM 37:7 NKJV

*In quietness and in confidence
shall be your strength.*
ISAIAH 30:15 KJV

MORE THOUGHTS
ABOUT LISTENING TO GOD

If you, too, will learn to wait upon God, to get alone with Him, and remain silent so that you can hear His voice when He is ready to speak to you, what a difference it will make in your life!

KAY ARTHUR

God's voice is still and quiet and easily buried under an avalanche of clamor.

CHARLES STANLEY

When God speaks to us, He should have our full attention.

BILLY GRAHAM

Prayer is not monologue, but dialogue. God's voice in response to mine is its most essential part.

ANDREW MURRAY

Nothing can calm our souls more, or better prepare us for life's challenges, than time spent alone with God.

BILLY GRAHAM

REMEMBER THIS

Prayer is two-way communication with God. Talking to God isn't enough; you should also listen to Him. He has many things He wants to tell you. The better you listen, the more you'll learn.

GET PRACTICAL

If you want to have a meaningful conversation with God, don't make Him shout. Instead, go to a quiet place and listen. If you keep listening long enough and carefully enough, the Lord will talk directly to you.

—⚬—

A CONVERSATION STARTER

Talk to a friend about the ways that God speaks to His believers.

NOTES TO YOURSELF
LISTENING TO GOD

Write down your favorite places to read the Bible, to pray, and to contemplate God's plans for your life.

15

THE QUESTION

Things that happened a long time ago still bother me. And, some of the things I see happening around me are very hard to accept. What should I do?

THE ANSWER

Whenever you encounter situations that you cannot change, you must learn the wisdom of acceptance. And you must learn to trust God. Simply do your best, and trust God to do the rest.

Don't waste today's time cluttering up tomorrow's opportunities with yesterday's troubles.

BARBARA JOHNSON

ACCEPTANCE

*For now we see in a mirror, dimly, but then
face to face. Now I know in part, but then
I shall know just as I also am known.*
1 CORINTHIANS 13:12 NKJV

Sometimes, we must accept life on its terms, not our own. Life has a way of unfolding, not as we will, but as it will. And sometimes, there is little we can do to change things. All of us must, from time to time, endure days filled with suffering and pain. And as human beings with limited understanding, we can never fully understand the plans of our Father in heaven. But as believers in a benevolent God, we must always trust Him, knowing that His love for us is eternal. So we must entrust the things we cannot change to our Creator. Once we have done so, we can prayerfully and faithfully tackle the important work that He has placed before us: the things we can change.

If you've encountered unfortunate circumstances that are beyond your power to control, accept those circumstances. And trust God. When you do, you can be comforted in the knowledge that your Creator is good, that His love endures forever, and that He understands His plans perfectly, even when you do not.

MORE FROM GOD'S WORD

Should we accept only good things from
the hand of God and never anything bad?
Job 2:10 NLT

Trust in the Lord with all your heart and
lean not on your own understanding.
Proverbs 3:5 NIV

For Yahweh is good, and His love is eternal;
His faithfulness endures through all generations.
Psalm 100:5 HCSB

He is the Lord. He will do what He thinks is good.
1 Samuel 3:18 HCSB

Everything God made is good, and nothing
should be refused if it is accepted with thanks.
1 Timothy 4:4 NCV

MORE THOUGHTS
ABOUT ACCEPTANCE

One of the marks of spiritual maturity is the quiet confidence that God is in control, without the need to understand why he does what he does.

CHARLES SWINDOLL

Acceptance says, "True, this is my situation at the moment. I'll look unblinkingly at the reality of it. But, I'll also open my hands to accept willingly whatever a loving Father sends."

CATHERINE MARSHALL

Accept each day as it comes to you. Do not waste your time and energy wishing for a different set of circumstances.

SARAH YOUNG

Christians who are strong in the faith grow as they accept whatever God allows to enter their lives.

BILLY GRAHAM

Loving Him means the thankful acceptance of all things that His love has appointed.

ELISABETH ELLIOT

REMEMBER THIS

Whenever you encounter situations that you cannot change, you must learn the wisdom of acceptance. And you must learn to trust God.

GET PRACTICAL

Think of at least one aspect of your life that you've been reluctant to accept, and then ask God to help you trust Him more by accepting the past.

—⁓—

A CONVERSATION STARTER

Talk to a friend about the wisdom required to accept things that cannot be changed.

NOTES TO YOURSELF
ABOUT ACCEPTANCE

Make a list of things you still worry about but cannot change. Then pray about your list.

16

THE QUESTION

It's hard for me to forgive the people who have hurt me. What does the Bible say about that?

THE ANSWER

God's Word instructs you to forgive others, no exceptions. Forgiveness is its own reward and bitterness is its own punishment, so guard your words and your thoughts accordingly.

He who cannot forgive others breaks the bridge over which he himself must pass.

Corrie ten Boom

THE POWER OF
FORGIVENESS

And be kind to one another, tenderhearted,
forgiving one another, just as God
in Christ forgave you.

EPHESIANS 4:32 NKJV

Have you experienced something so painful, so hurtful, so intense that your life was forever changed? And do you blame someone else for the pain? If so, it's time to imitate Christ on the cross. It's time to forgive.

Forgiveness is a gift of great value, but ironically it's a gift that is often worth more to the giver than to the recipient. You simply cannot give the gift of forgiveness without receiving an important blessing for yourself.

From a psychological perspective, the act of forgiving relieves you of some very heavy mental baggage: persistent feelings of hatred, anger, and regret. More importantly, the act of forgiveness brings with it a spiritual blessing, a knowledge that you have honored your heavenly Father by obeying His commandments.

Simply put, forgiveness is a gift that you give yourself by giving it to someone else. When you make the choice to forgive, everybody wins, including you.

MORE FROM GOD'S WORD

The merciful are blessed, for they
will be shown mercy.
MATTHEW 5:7 HCSB

Judge not, and you shall not be judged.
Condemn not, and you shall not be condemned.
Forgive, and you will be forgiven.
LUKE 6:37 NKJV

And whenever you stand praying, if you
have anything against anyone, forgive him,
so that your Father in heaven may also
forgive you your wrongdoing.
MARK 11:25 HCSB

But I say to you, love your enemies
and pray for those who persecute you.
MATTHEW 5:44 NASB

Above all, love each other deeply, because love
covers over a multitude of sins.
1 PETER 4:8 NIV

MORE THOUGHTS ABOUT FORGIVENESS

*In one bold stroke, forgiveness obliterates the past
and permits us to enter the land of new beginnings.*

BILLY GRAHAM

*Forgiveness is one of the most beautiful words in
the human vocabulary. How much pain could be
avoided if we all learned the meaning of this word!*

BILLY GRAHAM

Forgiveness is God's command.

MARTIN LUTHER

*Forgiveness does not change the past,
but it does enlarge the future.*

DAVID JEREMIAH

*Forgiveness is an act of the will,
and the will can function regardless of the
temperature of the heart.*

CORRIE TEN BOOM

REMEMBER THIS

God commands us to love all people, regardless of their personality styles. So don't be quick to judge others. Instead be quick to forgive them.

GET PRACTICAL

Make a list of the people you still need to forgive. Then ask God to cleanse your heart of bitterness, animosity, and regret. If you ask Him sincerely and often, He will respond.

—ᴧᴧ—

A CONVERSATION STARTER

Talk to a friend about the rewards of forgiving and the costs of not forgiving.

NOTES TO YOURSELF
ABOUT FORGIVENESS

Make a list of people you need to forgive today.

17

THE QUESTION

It seems like I'm constantly bumping into somebody with a prickly personality. Why do I seem to encounter so many difficult people?

THE ANSWER

We can never be sure why God allows us to encounter difficult people. But we can be certain He has a plan for our lives that includes the spiritual growth that inevitably occurs when we learn how to deal with difficult people and troubling situations.

———⚍———

And we know that God causes all things to work together for good to those who love God, to those who are called according to His purpose.

ROMANS 8:28 NASB

WE ALL DEAL WITH DIFFICULT PEOPLE

Bad temper is contagious—don't get infected.

PROVERBS 22:25 MSG

When you encounter a difficult person, it's up to you, and nobody else, to maintain your peace mind. Of course, the other person's prickly personality may make your job harder. After all, difficult people have a way of riling our emotions and distorting our thoughts. But with God's help, and with a little common sense, we can find peace amid the emotional storm.

Life is too short to allow another person's problematic personality to invade your psyche and ruin your day. But because human emotions are contagious, there's always the danger that you'll be drawn into the other person's mental state, with predictably negative consequences.

A far better strategy is to step back from the situation, say a silent prayer, and ask God to help you retain a sense of calm. When you do, He'll answer your prayer. The storm will pass, and you'll be glad you retained your emotional stability, even though the people around you were losing theirs.

MORE FROM GOD'S WORD

A perverse person stirs up conflict,
and a gossip separates close friends.
PROVERBS 16:28 NIV

Stay away from a foolish man; you will
gain no knowledge from his speech.
PROVERBS 14:7 HCSB

A person with great anger bears the penalty;
if you rescue him, you'll have to do it again.
PROVERBS 19:19 HCSB

Don't make friends with an angry man, and don't
be a companion of a hot-tempered man, or you
will learn his ways and entangle yourself in a snare.
PROVERBS 22:24-25 HCSB

Mockers can get a whole town agitated,
but those who are wise will calm anger.
PROVERBS 29:8 NLT

MORE THOUGHTS ABOUT DEALING WITH DIFFICULT PEOPLE

If you are a Christian, you are not a citizen of this world trying to get to heaven; you are a citizen of heaven making your way through this world.

VANCE HAVNER

How often should you forgive the other person? Only as many times as you want God to forgive you!

MARIE T. FREEMAN

Whatever a person may be like, we must still love them because we love God.

JOHN CALVIN

We are all fallen creatures and all very hard to live with.

C. S. LEWIS

Give me such love for God and men as will blot out all hatred and bitterness.

DIETRICH BONHOEFFER

REMEMBER THIS

For the rest of your life, you'll encounter people with prickly personalities, so you might as well learn how to deal with them now. You can take comfort in the fact that, with God's help, you can learn how to deal with difficult personalities in ways that are pleasing to Him and helpful to you.

GET PRACTICAL

Think of several people you know who have prickly personalities. How have you dealt with them in the past? How should you deal with them in the future?

—⧜—

A CONVERSATION STARTER

Talk to a friend about better ways to deal with difficult people.

NOTES TO YOURSELF
DEALING WITH
DIFFICULT PEOPLE

Write down the ways that you typically respond to people with difficult personalities. What are the positive aspects of your typical response? What are the negative aspects?

18

THE QUESTION

I know that everybody has tough times, but lately it seems like I've had more than my share. When circumstances unfold in ways that are unfortunate, or even tragic, how should I respond?

THE ANSWER

When tough times arrive (and they will), you should work as if everything depended on you and pray as if everything depended on God. And remember that a change of circumstances is rarely as important as a change in attitude.

Don't waste energy regretting the way things are or thinking about what might have been. Start at the present moment—accepting things exactly as they are—and search for My way in the midst of those circumstances.

SARAH YOUNG

LIVING ABOVE OUR CIRCUMSTANCES

Trust in him at all times, you people; pour out your hearts to him, for God is our refuge.

PSALM 62:8 NIV

From time to time, all of us must endure circumstances that try our souls and stir up our emotions. We find ourselves in situations that we didn't ask for and probably don't deserve. During these times, we try our best to "hold up under the circumstances." But God has a better plan. He intends for us to rise above our circumstances, and He's promised to help us do it.

On many occasions, our outer struggles are simply manifestations of the inner conflicts that we feel when we stray from God's path. What's needed is a refresher course in God's promise of peace. When we read God's Word, we discover that peace is possible if we obey Him and follow in the footsteps of His Son.

Are you dealing with a difficult situation or a tough problem? Do you struggle with occasional periods of discouragement and doubt? Are you worried, weary, or downcast? If so, don't face tough times alone. Face them with God as your partner, your protector, and your guide. When you do, He will give you the strength to meet any challenge, the courage to face any problem, and the patience to endure any circumstance.

MORE FROM GOD'S WORD

*I have learned in whatever state I am,
to be content.*
PHILIPPIANS 4:11 NKJV

*Cast your burden on the LORD, and He
shall sustain you; He shall never permit
the righteous to be moved.*
PSALM 55:22 NKJV

*God is our protection and our strength.
He always helps in times of trouble.*
PSALM 46:1 NCV

*The LORD is a refuge for the oppressed,
a refuge in times of trouble.*
PSALM 9:9 HCSB

*The LORD is a refuge for His people
and a stronghold.*
JOEL 3:16 NASB

MORE THOUGHTS ABOUT LIVING ABOVE OUR CIRCUMSTANCES

Every experience God gives us, every person he brings into our lives, is the perfect preparation for the future that only he can see.

CORRIE TEN BOOM

Jesus did not promise to change the circumstances around us. He promised great peace and pure joy to those who would learn to believe that God actually controls all things.

CORRIE TEN BOOM

No matter what our circumstance, we can find a reason to be thankful.

DAVID JEREMIAH

Don't let obstacles along the road to eternity shake your confidence in God's promises.

DAVID JEREMIAH

Subdue your heart to match your circumstances.

JONI EARECKSON TADA

REMEMBER THIS

A change of circumstances is rarely as important as a change in attitude. If you change your thoughts, you will most certainly change your circumstances.

GET PRACTICAL

With Christ you don't have to do the best you can "under the circumstances." With Him, you can rise "above the circumstances." Think of at least one thing you can begin today to rise above your current circumstances.

—∿—

A CONVERSATION STARTER

Talk to a friend about the lessons you both can learn from difficult circumstances.

NOTES TO YOURSELF
ABOUT LIVING ABOVE OUR CIRCUMSTANCES

Write down your thoughts about better, more effective ways to deal with difficult circumstances.

19

THE QUESTION

Sometimes, it's hard to know exactly what to do. What does the Bible say about following my conscience?

THE ANSWER

God's Word teaches that the little voice inside your head will guide you down the right path if you listen carefully. Very often, your conscience will actually tell you what God wants you to do. So listen, learn, and behave accordingly.

Conscience is our wisest counselor and teacher, our most faithful and most patient friend.

BILLY GRAHAM

LISTENING TO YOUR CONSCIENCE

Now the goal of our instruction is love from a pure heart, a good conscience, and a sincere faith.

1 Timothy 1:5 HCSB

God has given each of us a conscience, and He intends for us to use it. But sometimes we don't. Instead of listening to that quiet inner voice that warns us against disobedience and danger, we're tempted to rush headlong into situations that we soon come to regret.

God promises that He rewards good conduct and that He blesses those who obey His Word. The Lord also issues a stern warning to those who rebel against His commandments. Wise believers heed that warning. Count yourself among their number.

Sometime soon, perhaps today, your conscience will speak; when it does, listen carefully. God may be trying to get a message through to you. Don't miss it.

MORE FROM GOD'S WORD

Behold, the kingdom of God is within you.
Luke 17:21 KJV

*People's thoughts can be like a deep well,
but someone with understanding can find
the wisdom there.*
Proverbs 20:5 NCV

*Create in me a clean heart, O God;
and renew a right spirit within me.*
Psalm 51:10 KJV

*Let us come near to God with a sincere heart and
a sure faith, because we have been made free
from a guilty conscience, and our bodies have
been washed with pure water.*
Hebrews 10:22 NCV

*So I strive always to keep my conscience
clear before God and man.*
Acts 24:16 NIV

MORE THOUGHTS ABOUT LISTENING TO YOUR CONSCIENCE

It is neither safe nor prudent to do anything against conscience.

MARTIN LUTHER

God speaks through a variety of means. In the present God primarily speaks by the Holy Spirit, through the Bible, prayer, circumstances, and the church.

HENRY BLACKABY

Conscience can only be satisfied if God is satisfied.

C. H. SPURGEON

The conscience is a built-in warning system that signals us when something we have done is wrong.

JOHN MACARTHUR

Conscience is God's voice to the inner man.

BILLY GRAHAM

REMEMBER THIS

God gave you a conscience for a very good reason: to use it. That's why it's vitally important that you learn to trust the quiet inner voice that God has placed in your heart.

GET PRACTICAL

When your conscience speaks, listen carefully. If you consistently live in accordance with your beliefs, God will guide your steps.

—ﬗ—

A CONVERSATION STARTER

Talk to a friend about the emotions, the distractions, and the temptations that can interfere with your ability to hear the quiet inner voice of your conscience.

NOTES TO YOURSELF
LISTENING TO YOUR CONSCIENCE

Write down your thoughts about listening to your conscience in everyday life.

....

....

....

....

....

....

....

....

....

....

....

20

THE QUESTION

I know that I'm not wise enough or strong enough
to make it on my own. I need God. If I want
Him to guide me, what should I do?

THE ANSWER

When dealing with your emotions, or anything else
for that matter, God's Word is the final word.
If you want God's guidance, ask for it. When you
pray for guidance, God will give it.

*Keep asking, and it will be given to you.
Keep searching, and you will find. Keep knocking,
and the door will be opened to you.
For everyone who asks receives, and the one
who searches finds, and to the one who knocks,
the door will be opened.*

MATTHEW 7:7-8 HCSB

LET GOD BE YOUR GUIDE

Trust in the LORD with all your heart, and lean not on your own understanding; in all your ways acknowledge Him, and He shall direct your paths.

PROVERBS 3:5-6 NKJV

When you find yourself caught up in an emotionally charged situation, ask God for guidance. Otherwise, you may find yourself caught up in an emotional outburst that results in bitter consequences.

God does not reward undisciplined behavior nor does He endorse impulsive outbursts. Instead, He instructs us to be mature, thoughtful, peaceful, and patient. Yet these qualities may not come naturally for most of us, so we need His help. When we petition Him in prayer, sincerely and often, He helps us reel in the negative emotions that, left unchecked, rob us of happiness and peace.

When we ask for God's guidance, with our hearts and minds open to His direction, He will lead us along a path of His choosing. But for many of us, listening to God is hard. We have so many things we want, and so many needs to pray for, that we spend far more time talking at God than we do listening to Him.

Corrie ten Boom observed, "God's guidance is even more important than common sense. I can declare that the deepest darkness is outshone by the light of Jesus." These words remind us that life is best lived when we seek the Lord's direction early and often.

Our Father has many ways to make Himself known. Our challenge is to make ourselves open to His instruction. So, if you're unsure of your next step, trust God's promises and talk to Him often. When you do, He'll guide your steps today, tomorrow, and forever.

MORE FROM GOD'S WORD

Morning by morning he wakens me and opens my understanding to his will. The Sovereign Lord has spoken to me, and I have listened.

ISAIAH 50:4-5 NLT

Teach me to do Your will, for You are my God; Your Spirit is good. Lead me in the land of uprightness.

PSALM 143:10 NKJV

Shew me thy ways, O Lord; teach me thy paths. Lead me in thy truth, and teach me: for thou art the God of my salvation; on thee do I wait all the day.

PSALM 25:4-5 KJV

The Lord says, "I will guide you along the best pathway for your life. I will advise you and watch over you."

PSALM 32:8 NLT

Yet Lord, You are our Father; we are the clay, and You are our potter; we all are the work of Your hands.

ISAIAH 64:8 HCSB

MORE THOUGHTS ABOUT GOD'S GUIDANCE

When we are obedient, God guides our steps and our stops.

CORRIE TEN BOOM

As you walk through the valley of the unknown, you will find the footprints of Jesus both in front of you and beside you.

CHARLES STANLEY

The will of God will never take us where the grace of God cannot sustain us.

BILLY GRAHAM

God never leads us to do anything that is contrary to the Bible.

BILLY GRAHAM

Are you serious about wanting God's guidance to become a personal reality in your life? The first step is to tell God that you know you can't manage your own life; that you need his help.

CATHERINE MARSHALL

REMEMBER THIS

When you form a genuine partnership with God, you can do amazing things. So make God your partner in every aspect of your life, including the way you handle your emotions.

GET PRACTICAL

If you want God's guidance, ask for it. When you pray for guidance, the Lord will give it. He will guide your steps if you let Him. Let Him.

—∾—

A CONVERSATION STARTER

Talk to a friend about specific ways you can hear God's voice and follow His path.